modern readers   stage 4

The Web

Eduardo Amos
Elisabeth Prescher
Ernesto Pasqualin

2nd edition

 Richmond

© EDUARDO AMOS, ELISABETH PRESCHER, ERNESTO PASQUALIN, 2004

Q Richmond

Diretoria: *Paul Berry*
Gerência editorial: *Sandra Possas*
Coordenação de revisão: *Estevam Vieira Lédo Jr.*
Coordenação de produção gráfica: *André Monteiro, Maria de Lourdes Rodrigues*
Coordenação de produção industrial: *Wilson Troque*

Projeto editorial: *Véra Regina A. Maselli, Kylie Mackin*

Assistência Editorial: *Gabriela Peixoto Vilanova*
Revisão: *Letras e Ideias Ass. em Textos*
Projeto gráfico de miolo e capa: *Ricardo Van Steen Comunicações e Propaganda Ltda./Oliver Fuchs*
Edição de arte: *Christiane Borin*
Ilustrações de miolo e capa: *Rogério Borges*
Diagramação: *EXATA Editoração*
Pré-impressão: *Helio P. de Souza Filho, Marcio H. Kamoto*
Impressão e acabamento: Log&Print Gráfica e Logística S.A.
Lote: 770808
Código: 12037207

Dados Internacionais de Catalogação na Publicação (CIP)
(Câmara Brasileira do Livro, SP, Brasil)

Amos, Eduardo
    The web / Eduardo Amos, Elisabeth Prescher,
Ernesto Pasqualin ; [ilustrações Rogério Borges] .
— 2. ed. — São Paulo : Moderna, 2003. —
(Modern readers ; stage 4)

    1. Inglês (Ensino fundamental) I. Prescher,
Elisabeth. II. Pasqualin, Ernesto. III. Borges,
Rogério. IV. Título. V. Série.

03-3401   CDD-372.652

Índices para catálogo sistemático:
1. Inglês : Ensino fundamental   372.652

ISBN 85-16-03720-7

Reprodução proibida. Art.184 do Código Penal e Lei 9.610 de 19 de fevereiro de 1998.

Todos os direitos reservados.

RICHMOND
SANTILLANA EDUCAÇÃO LTDA.
Rua Padre Adelino, 758, 3ª andar — Belenzinho
São Paulo — SP — Brasil — CEP 03303-904
www.richmond.com.br
2023

Impresso no Brasil

Sharon hurried into the dressing room. She was late. Marilyn was there finishing her make-up.

"Did you see my necklace, Sharon?" asked Marilyn.

"What necklace?"

"The pearl necklace. It was right here on my table. I can't find it."

"Did you look in the drawers?" asked Sharon.

"Yes, but there's no sign of it."

"Well, you can take my necklace," said Sharon. "We'll look for your necklace after the show."

"Thanks," Marilyn said. "Listen! I saw Bruce waiting for you outside."

"Oh, no! Mrs Carson doesn't like him. I'll tell him to go away."

Sharon and Marilyn were students at Sunset Hill High School and worked part-time for Mrs Carson's modeling agency. They were working at a fashion show, modeling a famous designer's new collection.

The next afternoon, the two girls went jogging at Sunset Park. Sharon's boyfriend, Bruce, and his best friend, Danny, were waiting for them at Joe's Café in the park.

"Are you sure you took the necklace to the fashion show last night?" Sharon was asking Marilyn as they approached the boys' table.

"I'm positive," answered Marilyn.

"Do you think someone stole it?" asked Sharon.

"I think so," Marilyn said. "One minute it was there, the next minute it was gone!"

"Don't you two have anything else to talk about?" said Bruce rudely. "All you do is talk about that stupid necklace!" Then he stood up and ran off to the jogging lane.

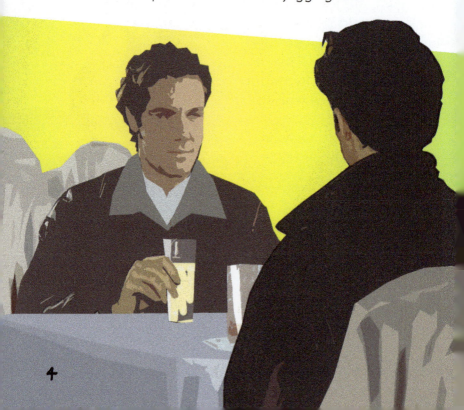

4

"What's the matter with him, Sharon?" asked Danny.
"I don't know. Bruce has changed a lot. He's different now."
"What do you mean, different?" Danny asked.
"I don't know. He's not the same person anymore."
"Perhaps it's because of the game tomorrow," suggested Danny.
"I don't think so," Sharon said. "He's the best player on the team."
"I still think he's worried about the game," said Danny.

The high school gym was crowded the next day. The Falcons were winning, and the crowd was screaming and shouting enthusiastically.

The Bears were losing, but playing fair. Towards the end of the game, Bruce hit one of the Bears in the eye and was sent off.

"What's the matter with Bruce O'Keefe?" asked Coach Rogers. "I can't believe he did that."

"I think he lost control again," said Coach Taylor.

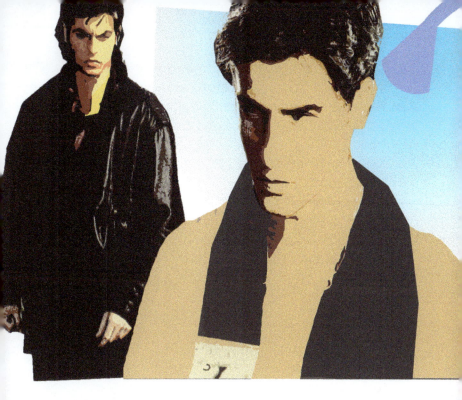

Minutes later, Bruce was taking a shower in the locker room when a skinny boy in a black leather jacket approached him.

"Going home early tonight, Champ?"

"Gus! What are you doing here?" Bruce said angrily. "I told you not to talk to me at school!"

"I came for the money."

"You know I don't have it yet."

"Your problem, buddy!" Gus said sarcastically. "The Warriors are after me for the money. I'll have to tell them you don't have it."

"Come on, Gus," begged Bruce. "You can't do that to me."

"Can't I?" Gus sounded angry now. "You either pay the fifty bucks, or else..."

"Or else?"

"Or else I'll tell the Warriors to collect the money directly from you," shouted Gus.

7

Before basketball practice the following afternoon, the Falcons were listening to their coaches. Coach Rogers was very serious. He was looking angrily at Bruce.

"O'Keefe, what you did yesterday was inexcusable!"

"But coach, I..."

"This is the second time you have lost control," interrupted Coach Rogers. "We don't want violent players on our team. I'm going to suspend you for the next three games."

"But, coach, that's till the end of the championship!" cried Bruce desperately.

"You asked for it, O'Keefe" added Coach Taylor. "We know you're our best player, but you're not our only one. Do you have anything to say?"

"No, just that I'm sorry. I would like to be on the team for the last games of the championship," answered Bruce.

"Not this time, O'Keefe," said Coach Taylor. "This time you have gone too far."

"Anything else?" Coach Rogers asked Coach Taylor.

"Yes. Patrick Doyle said that somebody stole twenty dollars from his wallet during the game yesterday. So, be careful with your belongings, everybody."

Rogers raised his eyebrows, looked at Taylor and said, "Okay, boys, let's practice. And you O'Keefe, get dressed and go home."

Bruce left school and went to Sharon's house. He was furious.

"What are you doing here so early?" asked Sharon.

Bruce told her what had happened at basketball practice.

"But Bruce, you were violent during the game!" she said softly. "What happened to the other player?"

"I don't care about him! Rogers suspended me till the end of the championship. It's not fair! I'm his best player."

"Why don't you talk to him again?" the girl suggested.

"No," replied Bruce. "I don't want to talk about it anymore. Anyhow, what time is your fashion show tonight?"

"At seven. Can you give me a ride?"

"Yeah. But I have to go to San Fernando first."

"San Fernando? That's not a very good neighborhood! What are you going to do there?" asked Sharon.

"That's my business, not yours," replied Bruce.

Bruce drove fast to a dark alley in San Fernando. He told Sharon to wait in the car and went into the alley. Sharon was hurt at what her boyfriend had said and waited silently.

A few minutes later, Bruce ran out of the alley, jumped into the car, and drove away as fast as he could. Minutes later, a police car stopped them.

Bruce had to show his driver's license and explain why he was driving so fast.

The police officer gave Bruce a speeding ticket and a long lecture on safe driving.

When they finally got to the fashion show, it was almost over. Sharon had missed her part.

"I think we have to talk, Sharon Bailey," said Mrs Carson when she saw the girl in the dressing room. "Come to my office tomorrow at three."

Mrs Carson had a respected modeling agency. Everybody liked her because she was fair and honest with her employees. Sharon was one of her youngest models. Mrs Carson liked her very much.

Sharon went to Mrs Carson's office and told her everything about the previous evening. The woman listened closely.

"I'm worried about your future," she said.

"My future?" Sharon asked. "But why?"

"Listen carefully, Sharon. Last night, three of the best fashion designers in the country came to our fashion show. They wanted to select some of my models for summer shows abroad."

"Oh, no!" cried Sharon. "That can't be true!"

"You missed your big opportunity."

"But Mrs Carson, I couldn't do anything."

"I know you couldn't," replied Mrs Carson. "Listen, Sharon! You're only sixteen and one of my top models. You're a beautiful and responsible girl. You have a brilliant career ahead of you."

"What are you trying to tell me?" asked Sharon.

"You missed last night's show because of your boyfriend. I've heard about him, and I don't like what I've heard."

"What do you mean?"

"Some of the models say that your boyfriend is on drugs. He smokes marijuana."

"What?" said Sharon surprised. "He doesn't even smoke cigarettes!"

"I don't know anything. That was what the girls heard at school," said Mrs Carson. "They also talked about Gus. You know that boy, don't you? Well, they say your boyfriend is close to him now."

"I don't believe it, Mrs Carson. It must be just gossip."

"Well, Sharon, it might be just gossip. But keep your eyes open! How well do you really know Bruce? Are you sure he's a nice boy?"

The woman stopped, looked at the girl for some time, and added, "I want you to know that I care about you. That's why I am telling you these things."

Sharon was confused when she left the agency. She couldn't believe what Mrs Carson had told her.

She wanted to talk to Bruce. She went home and called him from her father's office.

"I have to talk to you, Bruce. It's urgent."

"What's the matter?" her boyfriend asked.

"Why didn't you go to school this morning?"

"I got up late."

"And why didn't you meet me for lunch? I was waiting for you and..."

"Knock it off, Sharon!" he interrupted. "You said it was something urgent. What is it?"

Sharon started crying on the phone. Bruce waited for a while and then hung up. Sharon cried for a long time. She didn't know what to think or do. Then, she saw a pamphlet on her father's desk. She read it.

That night, Danny and Marilyn were driving past the shopping center.

"Look, Danny! It's Bruce, isn't it?" said Marilyn.

"Yes! What's he doing with the Warriors?"

"I don't know," Marilyn said. "I'm afraid for him, Danny. Let's talk to Sharon."

Marilyn and Danny met up with Sharon at Joe's Café. They told her what they had seen. Marilyn suspected Bruce was involved with drugs.

"Look, Marilyn," said Danny. "I know Bruce. He's my best friend. He's a nice guy, a good athlete. Maybe you're wrong. Maybe he is this way because he had another fight with his father."

"I'm afraid Marilyn's right, Danny," replied Sharon. "I read a pamphlet about drugs yesterday. Bruce shows all the symptoms described. He's nervous and aggressive. He loses control easily. He's losing weight. He doesn't care about anything. His eyes are constantly red and he refuses to talk about it."

"Is there anything we can do for him?" asked Marilyn.

"I tried to talk to him on the phone, but he hung up on me," said Sharon. "Maybe if you try, Danny…"

"I'll try," Danny said. "I'll talk to him."

Late that night, Mr O'Keefe saw lights on in the garage and went down to turn them off. Bruce's father was a successful executive in an automobile company, but he was quite irritable at home.

As he approached the garage, he noticed there was someone inside.

"Is that you, Bruce?" asked Mr O'Keefe.

When Bruce heard his father's voice, he quickly threw his jacket over something on the table.

"What are you doing here at this time of night?" asked Mr O'Keefe, opening the door.

"I was just looking for an old pair of sneakers."

"What for?"

"For basketball practice," said Bruce.

"Listen to me, Bruce," his father said angrily. "I'm not going to listen to your lies anymore. Coach Rogers told me you're off the team till the end of the championship. What do you think I am? Stupid?"

"But, Dad..." Bruce was really afraid now.

"Shut up!" shouted Mr O'Keefe. Then he picked up Bruce's jacket. "What's this?" he asked when he saw the tiny packages on the table.

Bruce just looked at the floor, totally petrified. Mr O'Keefe picked up one of the little white packages. He turned pale.

"Drugs!" he said in a low voice. "I can't believe it. My son involved with drugs!"

"But, Dad, I can..."

"Don't say anything!" he shouted. "You're not only taking drugs, you're selling them. You're a drug pusher. My God! My son is an addict and a drug pusher."

"But, Dad..."

"Shut up! Don't call me Dad. You're not my son any longer. I want you out of this house before morning. I don't want my family involved with an addict and a drug pusher. You don't belong here among decent people. I want you as far away as possible!"

"Are you sure I'm not going to bother you and your mother, Danny?" asked Bruce.

"Of course not," answered Danny. "This is my music studio. It's my place in the house. You can stay here till you decide what you're going to do."

"Did you tell your mother about me?"

"Sure I did. I told her everything."

"What did she say?"

"Look, Bruce. My mother thinks you need help. She said that maybe we can help you. But you have to make up your mind first."

"Thanks, Danny," said Bruce very touched. "I talked to Sharon, too. She also wants to help. I'm going to meet her at Joe's Café after school. Can you come too?"

"Of course, Bruce. I'll be there."

Hours later, at Joe's Café, a waiter handed Bruce a message.

"This is for you, Bruce," said the waiter.

"Who gave it to you?" asked Bruce.

"Someone I don't know," replied the waiter.

Bruce was reading the note when Sharon and Danny arrived.

"Are you all right?" asked Sharon.

"I guess so," answered Bruce showing the message to his friends. "Look!"

"What does it mean?" asked Danny.

"Zepellin is my code name," explained Bruce. "This message is from the Warriors. They want me to meet up with them tonight."

"You're working for the Warriors!" exclaimed Sharon.

"Yes, Sharon. I work for them."

"But Bruce, how did you get into all this?" asked Danny.

"Well, I owed them some money and couldn't pay. They forced me to make a delivery to pay back what I owed. That's how it started."

"Oh, Bruce," said Sharon. "Didn't you know this is the way it always starts?"

"Yes, I did, Sharon," answered Bruce. "But I didn't think it could happen to me... I thought I could handle it. I was sure I could quit any time. In the beginning, I just smoked marijuana. Then, I wanted to try cocaine. I started using it a lot. I started needing it."

His two friends just looked at him. Then Sharon said, "Now it makes sense. Marilyn's necklace,... the money stolen from the locker room. You... you really needed it, didn't you, Bruce?"

Bruce simply nodded in silence.

"Well, Bruce, is there anything we can do for you? Do you want to talk to a counselor?" asked Danny. "My mother has a great friend who works with kids involved in substance abuse. She's cool."

"Yeah, I think I'd like to meet her." Then he told his friends that he was planning to quit the Warriors. "I have paid my debt many times over. I'll tell them I'm going to quit. I want you to come with me and wait in the car just in case something goes wrong."

The three kids were tense as they drove to San Fernando that night. They knew that the Warriors were dangerous. They knew that it wouldn't be easy for Bruce to leave the group.

The car approached the Warriors' alley. It was very dark. Danny turned off the lights and parked the car.

Bruce was walking away from the car when they heard footsteps. Somebody was coming out of the alley. Danny quickly turned the headlights on. They were terrified to see Gus coming out of the alley. He was bent over and bleeding. The three of them ran to help him.

Gus fell on the ground before the kids could get to him.
"Gus! For God's sake! What happened?" cried Bruce.
"I just wanted to quit," Gus said and fainted.
"Let's get out of here!" shouted Bruce.

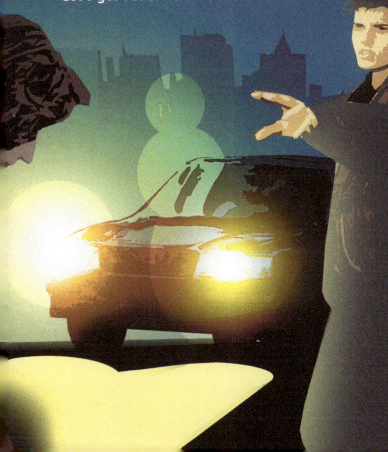

21

Danny drove fast through the dark streets till they reached Sharon's place. When they stopped, Sharon was the first to speak.

"Now what? Should we call the police?"

"No!" cried Bruce nervously. "How can we explain what we were doing there?"

"But Gus was bleeding a lot. He could be badly hurt," replied Danny.

"Maybe we can make an anonymous call and tell the police where he is," said Sharon.

"OK, but you do it," said Bruce. "I have to go."

"Oh, Bruce," cried Sharon. "Poor Gus is hurt, maybe dead. They'll try to hurt you too if they know you want to quit."

"Yes," said Bruce. "I was thinking about that too. I'm trapped."

"Bruce," said Danny. "I can't get Gus out of my mind. I think you're in serious trouble. Let's ask someone for help."

"I don't need anybody's help," shouted Bruce. "I have to go now. I have to think."

The next morning, the news about Gus's death was on the front page of the local newspaper. Everyone at school was talking about it. Everyone was shocked by the mysterious and violent way he had died.

Bruce was really frightened. He didn't go to the park. He didn't talk to his friends much. He didn't see the Warriors again. He spent most of his time at Danny's music studio.

A few days later, Gus's death was something of the past. Life went on and soon everybody was talking about Sharon's birthday the following week. Dr Bailey was going to give her a big party.

The following Saturday night, the Baileys' house was crowded with young people.

Sharon was beautiful in her new blue dress, but she was sad. She and Bruce hadn't talked much since that terrible night, but they couldn't forget it.

The party was really going strong at midnight. There was a lot of noise, singing, dancing and music playing.

Nobody heard them. Nobody saw them coming. All of a sudden, the Warriors were in the house.

They pushed, punched, kicked, and slapped the kids. Nobody escaped their rage.

Many people were badly hurt. Some were taken to hospital. Everyone was shocked. Nobody understood what had happened, nobody could explain such violence.

Only Sharon, Bruce, and Danny got the message.

Daybreak found the three friends sitting on the front porch. They were silent.

Sharon was sad. She thought about her party, her friends in hospital, her house half-destroyed. She thought about her career. She thought about Gus and what Bruce was doing with his life.

"Bruce," she whispered. "You have to make some decisions. I feel guilty about what happened to my friends and my parents' house."

"I feel guilty, too," said Danny. "I feel responsible for the fight and even for Gus."

"I know. I know that. Honestly," said Bruce. "But what can I do? I thought I could deal with things myself, but..."

"I love you, Bruce, but this is it for me. I'm not going to watch you destroy yourself and other people who really love you," said Sharon.

"Come on, Sharon..." said Bruce.

"Sharon is right, Bruce," interrupted Danny. "You have to make your choice. Think about what has happened so far. Coach Rogers suspended you from the team, Sharon missed a great career opportunity, your father threw you out of the house, your friends got hurt at the party, Sharon's house is a mess. Isn't that enough for you?"

"You have to make a choice, Bruce," said Sharon. "You either begin to cut drugs out of your life and look for help, or you become a Warrior."

"I don't want to be a Warrior! I want to stay with you, Sharon," shouted Bruce, tears in his eyes. "I want to be your friend, Danny. I love you, guys." He paused for a while, then said, "Yes, I need help. Please, help me."

Sharon put her hand on his head and said softly, "Calm down. I'll talk to my father right now. Wait here."

Sharon went into the house and called her father. They went to his office to talk. She started telling him everything. She told him about Bruce's behaviour at school and his involvement with the Warriors. She told him about Gus. She was crying when she finished.

Dr Bailey walked to the window and thought for a long time. Sharon just looked at him.

"Why didn't you tell me about this before, darling?"

"I'm sorry, Dad. Danny and I were just trying to help Bruce."

"Help? The boy is a pusher and you think you can help him?" said Dr Bailey. "You are risking your life!"

They were both silent. "Dad," Sharon asked, "do you think you can help him?"

"Help Bruce? But he's not my son. It's not my problem!"

"Whose problem is it, then?" asked Sharon.

"I don't know," said Dr Bailey.

"Oh, yes, you know, but you don't care. It's my problem. It's your problem. It's everybody's problem! Parents always think that this can't happen to their children. We, the kids, think that this can't happen to us. Drugs are something you just read about in the papers. Isn't that right, Dad? Isn't that right?"

"Calm down, Sharon," said Dr Bailey. "You know we can't save the world."

"All right, Dad. I know I'm acting like a child. But I love Bruce. And I'm going to try to help him!"

"No, you're not, Sharon. It's dangerous."

"Oh, Dad. I'm disappointed in you. Aren't you a doctor? Don't you know that drug addiction is a disease? When kids get caught up in the web, they need help. Bruce is sick, Dad!" Sharon shouted desperately.

Dr Bailey was touched by what his daughter had said. He hugged her tightly. There were tears in his eyes.

"Where's Bruce now?" he asked.

"Outside with Danny. I told them to wait."

"Tell them to come talk to me. Let's see what we can do."

Dr Bailey went to the telephone.

"Narcotics Division, please. Commissioner Connors? This is Dr Bailey speaking. I have to talk to you. It's urgent. I have serious reasons to believe that a boy may be killed. OK, see you in an hour."

— Sunset Chronicle

Drug gang busted in San Fernando

San Fernando — An important drug traffic connection was dismantled yesterday. With the help of a Federal Narcotics Officer, the local police arrested the leaders of a gang known as the Warriors in San Fernando.

Commissioner Connors said that the group was suspected of drug trafficking, robbery, vandalism and murder.

The San Fernando Police Department has been investigating the warriors since last December.

Information given by a youngster who had been involved with the gang provided the key to the success of the operation.

According to the Federal Narcotics Department, this arrest may lead to the disclosure of even more important information about the San Fernando connection.

Bruce was free from the Warriors' revenge. However, he was not free from the drug web.

He decided to go to a counselor and join a drug rehabilitation program.

The nightmare wasn't over, but he knew that with the help of good professionals and the love of Sharon and his friends, he could make a new start.

KEY WORDS

abroad (11) no exterior
addict (17) viciado
alley (10) beco
anymore (9) mais, nunca mais
approach, approached (7) aproximar-se de
arrest, arrested (31) prender
a while (13) um tempo
badly (22) gravemente
become (27) tornar-se
belongings (8) coisas
beg, begged (7) implorar
bent over (21) inclinado
bleeding (21) sangrando
bother (18) incomodar
bucks (7) dólares
buddy (7) cara
bust, busted (31) prender
care (13) importar-se
career (12) carreira
carefully (11) cuidadosamente
championship (8) campeonato
choice (27) escolha
closely (11) com atenção
coach, coaches (6) treinador(es)
cool (20) legal
counselor (20) conselheiro
crowd (6) multidão
crowded (6) lotado
daybreak (26) amanhecer
dead (22) morto
deal with (26) lidar com
death (23) morte

debt (20) dívida
delivery (20) entrega
designer (4) estilista de moda
disease (29) doença
drawer (3) gaveta
dressing room (3) camarim
driver's license (10) carteira de motorista
drug pusher (17) traficante de drogas
easily (15) facilmente
else (4) mais
eyebrow (8) sobrancelha
fashion (4) moda
feel (26) sentir
fight (14) briga, discussão
find (3) encontrar
footsteps (21) passos
forget (24) esquecer
frightened (23) assustado
get caught up (29) ficar preso
get dressed (8) vestir-se
go away (3) ir embora
gossip (12) fofoca
guilty (26) culpado
guy (14) rapaz, "cara"
half-destroyed (26) meio destruída
hang up, hung up (13) desligar
headlight (21) farol (de carro)
hear, heard (12) ouvir
hit, hit (6) bater
hug, hugged (30) abraçar

hurt (10) magoada
inexcusable (8) indesculpável
inside (16) dentro
jog, jogging (4) correr
jogging lane (4) pista de cooper
join (32) inscrever-se
keep (12) manter
key (31) chave
kick, kicked (25) chutar
kid (29) criança
killed (30) morto
leather (7) couro
lecture (10) palestra
lie (16) mentira
locker room (7) vestiário
lose, losing (15) perder
make-up (3) maquiagem
mess (27) bagunça
miss, missed (10) perder
murder (31) assassinato
necklace (3) colar
neighborhood (9) bairro
nightmare (32) pesadelo
nod, nodded (20) fazer que sim com a cabeça
or else (7) caso contrário
outside (3) lá fora
owe, owed (20) dever
pamphlet (15) folheto, panfleto
park, parked (21) estacionar
part-time (4) meio período
pearl (3) pérola
place (18) lugar
porch (26) varanda
practice (8) treino
punch, punched (25) socar
quit (20) abandonar

rage (25) fúria, raiva
raise, raised (8) levantar
reach, reached (22) chegar
refuse, refuses (15) recusar-se
revenge (32) vingança
risk, risking (28) arriscar
robbery (31) assalto
rudely (4) rudemente
safe driving (10) dirigir com cuidado
same (5) mesma
sarcastically (7) de forma sarcástica
save (29) salvar
scream, screaming (6) gritar
send off, sent off (6) expulsar
shocked (23) chocado
shout, shouting (6) gritar
sick (29) doente
since (24) desde
skinny (7) magricela
slap, slapped (25) dar tapas
smoke, smokes (12) fumar
sneakers (16) tênis
softly (9) suavemente
somebody (8) alguém
sound, sounded (7) parecer
speeding ticket (10) multa por excesso de velocidade
steal, stole (8) roubar
strong (24) movimentada, cheia
successful (16) bem-sucedido
suspend (8) expulsar
take, taking a shower (7) tomar banho
tear (27) lágrima
terrified (21) apavorado
think, thought (20) pensar

through (22) pelas
throw, threw (16) jogar, atirar
till (8) até
tiny (16) pequenos
touched (18) tocado, comovido
towards (6) próximo
trouble (22) encrenca
turn off, turned off (21) desligar
voice (17) voz
wait, waiting (3) esperar
waiter (19) garçom
wallet (8) carteira
way (14) jeito
weight (15) peso
whisper, whispered (26) sussurrar
win, winning (6) vencer
worried (5) preocupado
yet (7) ainda
youngster (31) jovem

Expressions

All of a sudden... (25) De repente
any longer.... (17) mais
be careful (8) tome cuidado!
Can you give me a ride? (9) Você pode me dar uma carona?
For God's sake! (21) Pelo amor de Deus!
He hung up on me! (15) Ele desligou na minha cara!
I can't get (...) out of my mind! (22) Não consigo tirar (alguém) da minha cabeça.
I guess so! (19) Acho que sim.
it makes sense! (20) faz sentido.
got the message (25) entenderam o recado.
keep your eyes open! (12) fique de olhos abertos.
Knock it off! (13) Pare com isso!
lost control (6) perdeu a cabeça.
make a new start (32) recomeçar
make up (one's) mind (18) decidir-se
Now what? (22) E agora?
That can't be true! (11) Não pode ser verdade!
That's my business, not yours! (9) É da minha conta, não da sua!
What do you mean...? (5) O que quer dizer...?
What for? (16) Para quê?
You've gone too far! (8) Você passou da conta.

ACTIVITIES

Before Reading

1. Look at the title and front cover of the book. What do you think "The Web" is about?

   a) the internet
   b) spiders
   c) the drug problem

While Reading

Pages 3-5

2. Read pages 3 and 4 and complete the sentences with the words from the box below:

   > collection   fashion show   modeling agency   make-up

   a) When Sharon entered the dressing room, Marilyn was finishing her _____ .
   b) Sharon and Marilyn worked part-time at a _____ .
   c) The girls were working at a _____ .
   d) They were modeling a new _____ .

3. Read pages 4 and 5. Who says these things? Write S (Sharon), M (Marilyn), B (Bruce) and D (Danny).

   a) (   ) "Are you sure you took that necklace to the fashion show last night?"
   b) (   ) "Don't you two have anything else to talk about?"
   c) (   ) "What's the matter with him, Sharon?"
   d) (   ) "I don't know. Bruce has changed a lot."

Pages 6 - 9

4. Read page 6 and complete the summary of the basketball game using the words in brackets.

> The gym _____ (be) crowded. The Falcons _____ (be/win) and the crowd _____ (be/scream) and _____ (shout). The Bears _____ (be/lose), but _____ (play) fair. Bruce _____ (hit) another player and _____ (be/send) off.

5. Read page 7 and put the conversation between Gus and Bruce in the right order (from 1 to 5).
   a) ( ) "Your problem, buddy!"
   b) ( ) "Come on, Gus," .... "You can't do that to me."
   c) ( ) "I came for the money."
   d) ( ) "Can't I?" [...] "You either pay the fifty bucks, or else..."
   e) ( ) "Or else I'll tell the Warriors to collect the money directly from you."

6. Read page 8 and correct these sentences so that they are true according to the text:
   a) Coach Rogers said that Bruce lost the game.
   b) Coach Rogers said he was going to suspend Bruce for four games.
   c) Coach Taylor said that someone stole twenty dollars from Patrick Doyle's wallet.

7. Read page 9 and decide whether these sentences are True (T) or False (F) according to the text.
   a) ( ) Sharon thinks that Bruce is violent during the game.
   b) ( ) Bruce agrees to talk to the coach.
   c) ( ) Sharon has to work tonight.

37

Pages 10 – 13

8. Look at the picture on pages 10 and 11. What do you think is happening?

9. Now read pages 10 and 11 and compare with what you wrote in 8.

10. Read pages 11 and 12 and decide whether these sentences are True (T) or False (F).
    a) (   ) Sharon missed an important opportunity.
    b) (   ) Mrs Carson heard that Bruce was on drugs.
    c) (   ) Sharon says that Bruce only smokes cigarettes.

11. Read page 13. What do you think?
    a) Why does Sharon start crying on the phone?
    b) What is the pamphlet about?

Pages 14 - 18

12. a) Look at the picture on pages 14 and 15. Describe the people.
    b) What do you think they are talking about?

13. Read and check your answers to 12.

14. On page 15, Sharon describes some symptoms of drug use which Bruce shows. Read and complete the table with these symptoms.

SYMPTOMS OF DRUG USE
1. He's nervous and aggressive.
2. He loses control easily.
3.
4.
5.

15. Read pages 16 to 18 and decide if the following statements are True (T) or False (F).

    a) (　) Mr O'Keefe calls Bruce an addict and a drug pusher.
    b) (　) Mr O'Keefe wants to help Bruce.
    c) (　) Danny's mother doesn't want Bruce in the house.

Pages 19 – 20

16. Look at the picture on page 19. Bruce receives a note. What does it say? Who is it from?

17. Read page 19 and compare with your answer to 16 above.

18. Answer these questions.
    a) Who is Zepellin?　　　　　b) Who are the Warriors?

19. Put these sentences in order (from 1 to 4) according to what Bruce says about his involvement with drugs.

    a) (　) "Then, I wanted to try cocaine."
    b) (　) "They forced me to make a delivery to pay back what I owed."
    c) (　) "In the beginning, I just smoked marijuana."
    d) (　) "I owed them some money and couldn't pay."

Pages 21 – 23

20. What happened to Gus? Why?

21. Who does these things? Write S (Sharon), B (Bruce), D (Danny).

    a) (　) suggests calling the police.
    b) (　) feels trapped.
    c) (　) wants to ask someone for help.
    d) (　) is going to have a party.

Pages 24 – 25

22. Look at the picture on page 24 and 25. What is happening?

23. Now read pages 24 and 25 and compare with your answer to 22.

Pages 26 – 30

24. Who does these things? Write S (Sharon), B (Bruce), D (Danny).
    a) (   ) feels guilty about what happened at the party.
    b) (   ) thought he could deal with things himself.
    c) (   ) says that he/she will talk to his/her father.

25. Are these sentences True or False?
    a) (   ) Dr Bailey thinks Sharon is in danger.
    b) (   ) Dr Bailey says that Bruce is not his problem.
    c) (   ) Dr Bailey doesn't agree to help.

Pages 31 – 32

26. Read the news story on page 31.
    a) What happened yesterday?
    b) Who was arrested?
    c) What crimes is the gang suspected of?

27. Read page 32 and decide: "Is Bruce free?"

After Reading (Optional Activities)

28. At first, Dr Bailey, Sharon's father, says that Bruce's problem is not his problem. Bruce's father sends him away.
    Do you agree with what they did? Whose problem is drugs? Hold a class debate.

29. Write a pamphlet warning young people about the use of drugs. Include:
    — the symptoms of drug use
    — how people get involved with drugs
    — help for people involved with drugs

30. **Mini-project:**
    Investigate the programs/associations in your neighborhood/city which help people involved with drugs.